A Guide to the Purchase

of

Children's Ponies

by

THE PONY CLUB ORGANISATION COMMITTEE

First Edition **1957**
Reprinted 1969

The British Horse Society
National Equestrian Centre
Kenilworth, Warwickshire, CV8 2LR

Published in 1977 by
BARRON'S
Woodbury, New York

Published in 1977 by
Barron's Educational Series, Inc.
113 Crossways Park Drive
Woodbury, New York 11797

Library of Congress Catalog No. 76-56351

Library of Congress Cataloging in Publication Data
Pony Club. Organisation Committee.
   A guide to the purchase of children's ponies.
   1. Ponies. 2. Horses—Buying. I. Title.
SF315.P65   1976   636.1'08'1   76-56351
ISBN 0-8120-0786-7

International Standard Book No. 0-8120-0786-7

CONTENTS

FOREWORD

IF A CHILD is to enjoy riding it is essential that he or she should be mounted sensibly, safely and suitably. A pony that is unsuitable for children is very difficult to get rid of once it has been purchased.

This book is produced in order to help those who are unfamiliar with the buying or selling of ponies. It is hoped that it will warn the intending purchasers against being exploited, and guide them in the choice of a suitable pony for their child.

Please note that in instances where the pronouns *he* and *him* appear, they have been used to avoid awkward prose. It should be understood that these references refer to *all* riders, whether male or female.

C. Guy Cubitt
Chairman
The Pony Club Organisation Committee

INTRODUCTION

BUYING PONIES FOR CHILDREN is a form of horse dealing. As such it is subject to all the risks and disappointments incidental to such transactions. The difficulties to be overcome in mounting a child successfully are no whit less than those encountered in mounting an adult.

No two ponies are alike in make, shape, or temperament, and the perfect pony does not exist. What may well seem near perfection to one child rarely proves equally so in the eyes of a subsequent owner since a similar degree of mutual affinity may not exist.

Mounting a child suitably calls for patience, prolonged search and thorough trial. But even when these conditions are fulfilled there remain the uncertain quantities of soundness, vice and price.

A pony is worth what he will fetch and no fixed scale of values exist. Safety and the right temperament must both be paid for and a suitable deal may well fall on the grounds of expense alone.

A good pony has been defined as one with many good, few indifferent and no bad points. A successful deal might equally well be defined as one in which there is some perfection, much satisfaction and little disillusion.

It is probably true to say that in horse dealing, more than in any other sphere of human activity we learn by our mistakes. A man who buys in error rarely buys a pony with the same fault a second time.

PART I
WHAT TO BUY

THE FIRST NECESSITY is to have an absolutely clear picture in mind as to just what sort of pony is required. Vague ideas such as 'Joan would love to have a pony' will get one nowhere.

In buying a pony, as in buying a motor car, certain conditions need to be fulfilled and certain requirements met. The parent in search of a pony should consider the problem under the following headings:

For what purpose is the pony required? *i.e.* CLASS
How big should the pony be? *i.e.* HEIGHT
How old should the pony be? *i.e.* AGE
What should he look like? *i.e.* MAKE AND SHAPE
How should he move? *i.e.* ACTION
How should he behave? *i.e.* TEMPERAMENT
Where is he to live? *i.e.* KEEP

Let us now consider each of the above in detail.

CLASS

The growing popularity of riding among children and with it the increasing demand for ponies for them, has led to the subdivision of ponies into various categories according to the class of work to which they are best suited. This classification, although still ill-defined, does however provide a useful guide to the parent in search of a pony and permits the choice, for the most part, to be narrowed down to the following:

Pets.   Strictly speaking these are outside the scope of this book since they are not true saddle ponies. However, a small child's first reaction to a pony is always to regard it more as a pet than as a utility animal. Furthermore, where love of the horse is an inherited instinct the possession of a pet pony goes a long way towards meeting a need.

On the whole ponies do not make good pets. Their keep is an expense and for the most part they are unresponsive to any advance which does not affect their stomachs. In any case the worst thing for any pony is idleness and a pony kept as a pet deteriorates when judged by any criterion.

Ponies intended as pets should be small. As such they are less terrifying to a small child. Age here is a matter of little importance. They must be docile and free of the vices of biting or kicking. However, in common with most of the animal kingdom, ponies exhibit to an uncanny degree a measure of docility in the presence of a small child which they do not always extend to grown-up people.

A Child's First Pony. As the name implies, this is a pony suitable as a child's first mount. The rider, being a novice needs the kind of pony that can be relied upon to instil confidence and to enable the development of riding abilities free of any fear of accident or mishap.

A 'First Pony' must therefore be one with experience, manners, the right temperament, and above all 'safe'. Inevitably such a pony cannot be young and here age is a matter of secondary importance, excepting only where the pony is required to serve in succession a line of brothers and sisters in due season. Indeed, an aged pony that knows his work makes an excellent first pony even if somewhat past his prime.

A 'Child's First Pony' may therefore be defined as one suited to a novice rider, on or off the leading rein, traffic proof and free of the vices of bolting, rearing, bucking or kicking.

A Child's Second Pony. A child that has learnt in some measure the control of a pony and has developed in some degree security in the saddle will sooner or later require remounting if knowledge is to be progressive. In short, the child will be due for a second pony.

The pony suitable at this stage must be one that will move on at the will of the rider at the pace desired, but which nevertheless is controllable at all times. Such a pony will call for a greater degree of control and a firmer seat on the part of the rider than he was capable of as a novice. Height, age, make and shape as well as temperament now all call for consideration since all directly affect the rider's performance and progress.

A 'Child's Second Pony' may be defined as one suitable for a child beyond the beginner's stage, but which is capable of control at all paces and free of the vices of bolting and rearing.

A Child's Hunter. This is a pony suitable for a child to ride to hounds across country. The pony, therefore, must provide a safe ride, be a good jumper and one which can be relied upon to behave properly in the presence of other people and hounds. Kickers or ponies addicted to kicking out at hounds are to be avoided.

Ponies which fall into this class vary greatly in height since even quite small ponies, capable of conveying a child safely across country, qualify for inclusion here.

A 'Child's Hunter' may be defined as one suitable for a child rider and which has been hunted with hounds, is capable of being hunted with hounds, and is free of the vices of kicking and bolting.

A Child's Show Pony. With the exception of the class of pet ponies mentioned, any of the ponies in the foregoing categories can be used as a show pony and indeed often are.

A true show pony, however, is one of such outstanding excellence in conformation, action, and temperament that it excels in competition with others in the show ring.

The majority of ponies which fall into this class are of the miniature thoroughbred type, the type most favoured by judges today. Their ultimate success, however, depends as much on their training, their action and their general performance as on actual looks.

Ponies of this class are inevitably expensive to buy and each further success in the ring enhances their value. In turn their enhanced value calls for higher standards of keep and management. In short they constitute a luxury article and their appeal lies chiefly in the direction of those whose interests are in the show ring.

A 'Child's Show Pony' may thus be defined as a pony of exceptional conformation, action, training and temperament which has won in show classes and is likely to win again.

A Child's Jumper.   This pony's sphere of usefulness lies in show jumping. They are judged by one criterion and one alone, namely their ability to jump big. Age, conformation and soundness count for little.

The increased popularity of show jumping and the provision now made for child jumpers has led to a demand for ponies of this category and they change hands at high prices on their performance record alone.

A 'Child's Jumping Pony' may be defined as one capable of being jumped at show standards and which has won prizes in jumping competitions.

A Child's Gymkhana Pony.   This pony is one whose special and only merit lies in success in gymkhana classes. Other uses, no doubt, it has too, but in the eyes of its owner, its value depends upon the winning of gymkhana events.

Such ponies are of any make, shape or height, their sole qualification being the complete indifference they exhibit to all forms of annoyance or disturbance, sacks, fireworks, wheel-barrows and what-not being taken as part of the normal incidents of life.

A 'Child's Gymkhana Pony' may be defined as a fast handy pony trained to lead and to stand, and one which has won prizes in gymkhana events.

The General Utility Pony. This rather nondescript pony is one designed to carry the whole family and to pull the tub cart too, if so required. He excels at nothing, but in his time plays many parts and serves one and all faithfully and well. Nevertheless, despised though he may be, he meets a need where conditions require that a large family must all share a single mount.

A pony that fills this role successfully may well prove a possession beyond price and win a love and affection from the many that is denied to the pony with a single owner.

For a pony so diverse in his activities no form of definition is possible.

HEIGHT

Height is a matter of first consideration in the purchase of a pony, if not actually of first importance. Any enquiry for a pony will inevitably solicit the rejoinder 'What height pony are you looking for?' It is for this reason that advertisements for ponies invariably carry a reference to height, whatever other particulars may be included or omitted.

Height has a double significance. It is in direct relationship to the under-or-over-mounting of a child, and has a further importance in regard to ponies intended for entering in show classes carrying a height limitation.

A pony on the small side is unsuitable for a tall long-legged child, as is also a large pony for a tiny tot. The latter may delight the ring-side crowd but the fact remains that the child is over-mounted.

Speaking in very general terms the following are the suitable height measurements in relation to a child's age, i.e. a child of average growth, height and build:

For a child under 7 years .. .. 10.3 hh. or less
For a child 7 – 9 years .. .. 11.00 to 12.00 hh.
For a child 11 – 13 years .. .. 12.00 to 13.00 hh.
For a child 13 – 15 years .. .. 13.00 to 14.2 hh.
For a child 15 – 17 years .. .. 14.2 to 15.2 hh.

An exception to the above must however be made in the case of heavily built, stocky ponies of the cob type, which will often carry a child, or even an adult admirably, notwithstanding a height measurement falling short of the above scale.

AGE

Age is of importance for two reasons. It directly affects the purchase price and value of the pony and it is also in immediate relationship to its expectation of life and working years.

A pony is mature at 5 years and in his prime at 6 years. The optimum age at which to buy is thus five years.

From birth up to five years a pony appreciates in value annually. From nine years he suffers depreciation, slight at first, but more rapid from 12 years of age onwards.

Ponies Underage. Ponies of three or four years of age are adolescent. As such they are unequal to the work required of a pony of mature age. The use of ponies of this age by children for hunting or a long day's work is to be deprecated and may even constitute cruelty. In any case, it implies that such were broken to saddle work far too young.

Their use in the show ring under saddle at this age is related to sale and future prospects, and not with a view to immediate use. Thus strictly speaking they constitute 'Likely to make' ponies and not 'Ponies suitable for a child'.

Parents are sometimes tempted to buy ponies of 3 or 4 years owing to the fact that at this age they are often very docile. Such docility, however, is related to adolescence and is no guide to temperament at maturity.

The purchase of ponies of tender age in the mistaken belief that 'it would be so nice for Joan and the pony to grow up together' creates a situation in which the blind are leading the blind to the ultimate discomfiture of both.

Overage Ponies. This is an entirely different matter. An overage pony with experience of his work often makes an excellent mount for a child, even though past his prime. At 14 years of age such may well have several years of useful life and work left in him. The prospective purchaser, however, needs to weigh carefully the objections to such a deal. It is almost certain, for one thing, that the money expended will never be recovered. Again the child may become very attached to the pony, but the expectation of life being short, its ultimate end will cause grief to all concerned. With increasing years the pony becomes less and less equal to the demands made by a progressive rider. An aged pony is more expensive to feed, does less well on his rations and may actually suffer if wintered out.

MAKE and SHAPE

Nobody wishes to own an ugly pony. Nor is there any need. Misshapen ponies, like misshapen riding clothes, are uncomfortable, often unsafe and may give rise to a feeling of inferiority in company with others. We cannot all have the best in ponies or riding clothes, but we can, at least, avoid deliberately purchasing the unsightly.

The subject of conformation is a vast one and quite beyond the scope of this book. Here we can only consider such aspects of make and shape as contribute to suitability, enjoyment, safety and comfort.

Round, fat tubby ponies make unsuitable saddle ponies for children. The gait, generally a waddle, is uncomfortable and a poor introduction to horsemanship. Such ponies stretch the legs of a small child to an undue degree and offer no security in the saddle. Furthermore, the saddle tends to slip round with disastrous results. Something reasonably narrow is greatly to be preferred, avoiding, however, the narrow-chested flat-ribbed pony.

A pony thick in the neck tires the arms of a small child and may even prove unmanageable. If in addition, as is often the case, the pony has the unpleasant habit of keeping the head low on the ground, the small rider must either become tired out or exasperated.

The withers are an important point in children's ponies. If ill-defined the saddle tends to slip forward onto the neck necessitating the use of a crupper to retain the saddle in position. The opposite defect, unduly prominent withers, create special difficulties and dangers in saddle fitting.

A pony long in the back never makes a good saddle pony, though this is of less consequence for harness work. A long back is not only unsightly but often results in the pony carrying light condition.

Misshapen quarters are a common feature of certain pony breeds and are to be avoided in that they constitute a weakness.

A pony narrow in the chest often proves an unsafe ride since the forelegs, being too close together, are liable to interfere with one another during progression. The same applies to a pony which moves close behind and particularly so where such is due to faulty hocks.

ACTION

By Action is understood the manner in which a pony moves at all paces, viz. walk, trot, canter and gallop. It is in direct relationship to the enjoyment of the ride and as such is a matter of great importance in the choice of a pony.

A pony with good action covers a maximum amount of ground with a minimum number of strides. Conversely, bad action involves a great amount of movement of the legs with little progression. A pony that moves well thus throws his feet forward at whatever pace he may be travelling and this is the point to be watched for when viewing a possible purchase.

Bad action shows in several ways. It may take the form of short stumpy steps or high lifting of the knees, such as is associated with harness ponies. Either is objectionable in a pony intended for saddle work.

Again faults in action may be limited to a single limb as when a pony throws a foot outwards or inwards during movement. Going close, either in front or behind, is another form of bad action as it may lead to self-inflicted wounds of the opposed leg.

TEMPERAMENT

Good temperament must be regarded as an essential qualification of a child's pony.

By temperament is understood a pony's demeanour under all conditions and circumstances. It is a matter of the utmost importance in the choice of a child's pony and in many cases may well be an over-riding consideration transcending every other aspect of the deal.

Good temperament implies docility, obedience, willingness and gentleness. These are by no means entirely an outcome of good breaking or training, but are rather part of its nature. Such characteristics inspire confidence in the child and promote advancement in knowledge of horsemanship for without confidence there can be no happiness in riding and without happiness in the saddle there can be no advance in knowledge.

The opposite characteristics and those to be avoided are obstinacy, fretfulness, independence amounting to disobedience, vice in one or other of its various forms and nappiness extending sometimes to treachery.

Ponies possessing the desirable characteristics are described as 'temperamentally suited to a child'.

KEEP

The choice of a pony is influenced materially by the manner in which the new pony is to be kept, namely in a stable or at grass. A pony which has been accustomed to stable life and particularly a well-bred pony, can scarcely be bought and turned out into a field to fend for himself.

Similarly, a pony which has been used to a life of liberty at grass may not take kindly to a stabled existence.

Ponies which have been kept at grass and which do well unstabled are advertised as 'Lives out'.

———————

PART II
WHERE TO BUY

THE FOLLOWING are the usual sources of supply of children's ponies:

By Purchase from Another Pony Club Member. Within a Branch of the Pony Club there are invariably ponies for sale, the most frequent reason for parting being 'Owner outgrown'.

This source of supply has much to recommend it. In the first place the record of the pony is known to all and its performance, whether at Pony Club rallies, hunting, as a jumper or for cross-country work, is open to observation. Further the pony is available within the district and in all probability no objection to trial arises. The opinion of the District Commissioner of the Branch on the suitability of the pony should also be forthcoming.

Some branches of the Pony Club maintain a list of ponies within their district which are for sale.

With a view to preventing any misunderstanding or the breaking of a friendship it is advisable always to have a pony purchased in this way submitted to veterinary examination before the deal is closed.

By Purchase from a Riding Establishment. Most riding schools combine horse dealing with their business and a regular turnover of ponies belonging to a school is the rule rather than the exception.

This also is an excellent source of supply since the pony under consideration is available for hire and thus for thorough trial before the deal is completed, thereby fulfilling one of the essential preliminaries to a satisfactory transaction. There is added safety too in the fact that no reputable riding establishment will knowingly become partner to a deal which will bring it discredit.

Some ponies which have been used to a riding school existence and to working in a string, are completely hopeless and nappy if taken out by themselves. It is well to make sure therefore that a prospective purchase from this source will go alone.

Ponies purchased from a Riding School always change hands somewhat above their true market value since the vendor is under necessity to make a profit on the deal as part of his legitimate business.

By Purchase through Sale Yards and Auctions. The majority of horses and ponies which change hands in this country are disposed of in this way. Usually the ponies are available for inspection beforehand, sometimes even on the day before the sale. Where the ponies offered at auction have been submitted to a veterinary examination beforehand, the certificate of such examination is 'lodged' with the auctioneers and is available for inspection.

Sometimes ponies auctioned under these conditions are sold on "warranty' but the period of availability of such warranty is always short and may even expire by 6 p.m. on the day of sale. Dissatisfaction with a pony bought at auction can only be redressed provided a 'breach of warranty' or 'fraud' can be established, and, in the case of breach of warranty only, within the period before its expiry as stated in the conditions of the sale.

Purchases made at auctions are necessarily something of a gamble unless the record of the pony happens to be known to the bidder beforehand. Gambling, however, operates in both directions and the possibility of acquiring a treasure at bargain prices is inherent in the transaction.

By Purchase by Advertisement.   The prospective purchaser advertises or answers an advertisement. The latter procedure is the more usual. The weekly paper *Horse and Hound* is the recognised medium for such advertisements in this country, although many provincial papers also carry useful livestock columns. Ponies advertised in a provincial paper are more likely to prove local.

In answering advertisements it is a good plan to call for a photograph. Such may often save a long and disappointing journey.

Ponies offered for sale by advertisement are not usually open to trial away from the vendor's premises since vendor and purchaser are unknown to each other. Permission to try out the pony on the vendor's premises, however, is a reasonable request and may reasonably be expected.

Ponies advertised as 'Open to any trial' are available for any fair trial by a prospective purchaser on the vendor's premises. Ponies advertised as 'Open to any examination' are available for examination by a veterinary surgeon appointed by either party.

PART III

HOW TO BUY

DISAPPOINTMENT, waste of money and misunderstanding can only be avoided, and then only in part, by strict adherence to the accepted method of procedure.

This is as follows:

CHOICE	— Make up your mind what you want
SEARCH	— Spend time and trouble looking for it
TRIAL	— When found investigate its possibilities
CERTIFICATION	— Buy after an inspection and certificate of a Veterinary Surgeon
PAYMENT	— Close the deal

The Choice.   Class, Height and Age call for attention first of all.   Conformation, Action and Temperament come into the picture later on.

Class.   The class of pony chosen lies for the most part in the classification already given.   For a beginner a 'First' pony is indicated. Children past this stage require a 'Second' pony. From there onwards the rider's special needs and interests influence the case whether they be hunting, jumping, showing or something else.

Height.   No vendor can produce a possible pony until some indication is given as to the height of pony the purchaser requires.

An immediate decision as to the approximate height of the pony required must thus be arrived at.

Age.   Age, too is an essential point if under-age or old ponies are not acceptable.

In short, the prospective purchaser clarifies the problem in some such form as this: 'Required a child's First pony, about 12.00 hands, not objected to if "aged" but preferably not over 14 years' or 'Required: A child's Second Pony, about 13.2 to 14.00 hands preferably six years of age or thereabouts'.

Choice having been settled all is in order to proceed to the next step.

The Search.   Having made up one's mind what to look for the next step is to search for it. The search for the right pony may well last as long as six months and generally speaking the more trouble taken in the matter the greater the satisfaction. Buy in haste and repent at leisure.

The most profitable fields for exploration have already been dealt with, but in all probability in the course of the search many a pony will be seen and many rejected. Such ought not to be regarded as so much waste of time for the effect of rejection is always to clarify in mind just exactly what is really required. Further, each rejection is in itself a gain in knowledge. Thus by a process of elimination the field is finally narrowed down to the 'possibles'.

The Trial.   The next step is a critical enquiry as to whether any of the 'possibles' can be regarded as a 'probable'. Conformation, Action and Temperament now come into the picture.

Conformation. The prospective purchaser views the pony for Make and Shape. Buying 'blind', that is to say without first viewing the pony, as in accepting a pony on advertisement, is at the best a risky procedure.

Action. If the general Make of the pony seems satisfactory he is then trotted up for Action.

Temperament. Finally he should be saddled and ridden for Temperament and enquiries made as to idiosyncrasies or vice.

For this important matter of Trial the purchaser, if inexperienced, will do well to take along with him some knowledgeable friend or experienced horseman to advise him. He should also take the child for whom the pony is intended. An essential part of Trial is that the pony shall be ridden by the parent or his adviser (provided the pony is large enough to carry an adult) and also by the child.

In cases in which the vendor provides a child to ride the pony, in all probability he will choose a child who can be relied upon to show off the pony to greatest advantage. Whilst such serves the useful purpose of indicating the pony's capabilities it is no guide as to how it will behave in the hands of the purchaser's own child. Thus the purchaser's child ought also to ride.

No difficulties usually arise in regard to Trial where purchase is from another Pony Club member or a local riding school. The trial of a pony from a distant riding establishment is normally only permitted on the owner's own premises. Little trial beyond viewing and trotting up is usually possible in the case of a pony bought at auction.

In certain circumstances vendors sometimes permit a pony to go to a prospective purchaser 'on a week's trial'. Such an arrangement would generally indicate good faith and that the deal is a genuine one. A prospective purchaser taking over a pony on such terms must be careful to submit the pony to fair trial only and to take such care generally of the animal as would a person of common prudence in looking after his own pony.

If the outcome of Trial is satisfaction and if it leaves the purchaser disposed to buy, then all is set for the next step in procedure and if such is included it is usual to make arrangements for this here and now.

Certification. This is 'vetting' and it comprises a critical enquiry as to whether the pony under review is physically fit or otherwise. It falls to the lot of the veterinary surgeon.

'Vetting', however, is by no means essential to the deal. Many a pony does in fact change hands without ever being 'vetted', the purchaser buying on his own judgement, on the pony's known record or in the belief that where ignorance is bliss 'tis folly to be wise as to such physical defects as exist.

Nevertheless, the certification of a pony is a step in purchase which ought not lightly to be omitted. An assurance that the pony is in fact fit, means much. On the other hand, it is well to know where one stands should certain disabilities come to light, and furthermore the purchase price is often reduced thereby. Again, it is just as important in a deal among friends as in a deal between strangers, since it provides the best possible safeguard against misunderstanding or a broken friendship.

A word of caution is necessary here. With the decline in the horse population of these Islands, not all veterinary surgeons today are actively engaged in equine practice. When employing a veterinary surgeon to examine a pony it is advisable therefore to choose some-one well versed in this class of work, even though he may not be the purchaser's regular veterinary surgeon for his other stock or domestic pets.

The act of Certification falls into two parts:

(1) Certification as to Identify and (2) Certification as to Soundness. It is usual for the examining surgeon to include both in a single certificate and in any case the latter is incomplete without the former.

Certification as to Identify.   Apart from the general description of the pony in the matter of colour and markings, this includes also a statement as to the animal's age and height measurement. Two important aspects of the deal are thus covered here.

Certification as to Soundness.   For the most part this covers the important aspects of vision, heart, wind, lameness, skin disease and condition. Forms of vice which undermine constitution are also included should they come to light.

A pony in which no physical disability is found is certified as 'Sound'. In all other cases the pony is reported to be 'Unsound', the reasons for rejection being incorporated in the certificate.

If the pony is Sound, then the purchaser can pass on at once to agreement as to price and the closing of the deal.

If, on the other hand, the pony is Unsound further consideration of the matter is necessary, namely the extent to which the defects noted (1) Detract from usefulness and (2) Detract from value.

Not all forms of unsoundness necessarily render a pony unworkable or unsafe. Every form of unsoundness detracts in some degree from value. The purchaser should seek the advice of the examining surgeon on the above two points and at the same time obtain his opinion for or against purchase.

Warranty.   This is a representation or statement made by a vendor regarding certain qualities of an animal offered for sale— usually its suitability and fitness for a certain class of work. Warranty is so seldom applied to children's ponies that it can be dismissed in a few words. Some sale yards offer warranty for ponies at auction, the terms of such being shown in the conditions governing the sale. No private vendor ordinarily offers terms of warranty.

Payment.   The last step in the deal. It is the custom in horse dealing that payment be made at the time the pony changes hands. This is wise and reasonable since anything may happen to the pony the moment it passes into new ownership. The price of the pony is the price as it stands when taken over and not what it looks like in three days' time.

It sometimes happens that a purchaser attempts to return a pony within a few weeks or even months of a deal on the grounds that it has not turned out to be all that was expected. The original owner is under no obligation to agree (except perhaps in the case of fraud). Should the original owner consent to 'take the pony back' then 'taking back' amounts to a new deal in the reverse direction and not to cancellation of the original contract. Such being the case the price may not be the same.

Sometimes a vendor attempts to bind down a purchaser to conditions such as 'Never to part with the pony' or 'To have the pony humanely destroyed in due course' or 'Never to sell the pony to a riding school'. It is questionable whether such arrangements are binding in law since the pony having changed ownership, becomes the property and part of the goods and chattels of the new owner. Such are better regarded as 'gentlemen's agreements'.

PART IV

THE PITFALLS

THESE, ALAS, are many and varied. No one, unfortunately, however experienced, is entirely free of the risk of making a mistake.
The risks for the most part arise directly from the fact that in horse
dealing we are concerned with the animate, in all its great diversity,
as distinct from the mechanical with its faithful reproduction of
type. Some consolation lies in the fact that the risks to be faced
possess a fascination peculiarly their own.

The following, though by no means an exhaustive list of the
many pitfalls awaiting the unwary, does for the most part cover
the more common forms of error.

DISHONESTY

The bad name associated with horse dealing is the direct result of
malpractices in the past. Although today dishonest dealing is far
less common than formerly it is still a hazard to be reckoned with.

In buying or selling anything a vendor is, generally speaking,
under no necessity to enlarge upon the shortcomings of the goods
offered. Similarly, in horse dealing. A man selling a pony is under
no obligation to enumerate its deficiencies and physical defects. It
is for the purchaser to find them out for himself.

Dishonesty only arises when someone makes statements which he knows to be untrue, e.g. that a pony never kicks, when he knows full well that it is a confirmed kicker; that the pony has never been lame, when it is subject to chronic lameness; or that a pony is six years of age when in reality it is fourteen. As it is extremely difficult to obtain redress in the case of a pony sold in bad faith, dishonest dealing nearly always leaves the unfortunate purchaser in the position of having to make the best of a bad bargain.

There are three safeguards against dishonest dealing, viz. (1) To deal only with someone whose reputation is a guarantee of a square deal; (2) To verify every statement made by the vendor about the pony; and (3) To obtain the independent opinion of a veterinary surgeon in regard to the pony's age, height and physical fitness.

VICE

Not all forms of vice are necessarily dangerous. All of them, however, are objectionable and detract from value. Some unfortunately are not detectable at the time of purchase. The following are the more common forms of vice in ponies of importance to parents. Purchasers are advised to check up on this list before closing a deal.

Difficult to Catch. The majority of children's ponies are kept at grass. The merits of this arrangement are completely nullified should it prove impossible to catch the pony when required. This matter is regarded as of such importance that owners offering a pony for sale advertise it as 'Easy to catch' or 'Comes when called' if they wish to indicate that it is free of this particular form of vice.

Jumping Out of the Field and Refusing to Live Alone. These may be considered together. A pony that refuses to settle down quietly in his field creates a problem. Through constant fretting he loses condition and in every attempt at gate-crashing the risk of barbed wire or stake injury is incurred. To provide a stable companion is only a part answer since the two may refuse to be separated when required separately for work.

Kicking, Biting, Nipping. All these are objectionable in children's ponies and dangerous too. Ponies free of these forms of vice are advertised as 'Quiet, in and out of the stable'.

Kicking Hounds. This form of vice is of importance only in regard to a pony used for hunting. However, as such it leads to ostracism and disgrace and renders a pony almost useless as a child's hunter.

Refusing to be Shod. This is a particularly irritating form of vice since it leads to the exasperation of all concerned, owner, child and blacksmith. Fortunately it is rare.

Refusing to Box. If it is the purchaser's intention to transport the pony to shows, Pony Club rallies, etc. by horse box or trailer he will do well to ensure that the pony is one that will enter a vehicle without protest.

Bucking. It is necessary to differentiate between 'Bucking' as a vice and 'Throwing a buck' in an exuberance of spirits. Most under-worked and over-fed ponies will throw a buck on occasions.

The confirmed bucker which seeks to unseat his rider without warning or provocation is an improperly broken and only part-trained pony and thus in effect not a made saddle pony at all.

Bolting. No form of vice to which ponies are addicted is more dangerous for a child. Fortunately also no form of vice in ponies is quite so rare. Such a pony is a totally unsafe ride for a child.

Shying. Shying is the exhibition of fright or nervousness in passing an unfamiliar object combined with a sideways jump away from it. The danger lies in the latter part since it may unseat the rider. Shying may arise from defective vision, be the result of a previous accident in similar connection or be pure naughtiness. Whatever the cause it is highly objectionable in a child's pony. Ponies free of the particular form of vice were formerly advertised as 'passes all road nuisances' but the term in common use today is 'traffic proof'.

Rearing. This is rare in ponies and arises through painful bitting or bad breaking.

FALSIFICATION OF AGE

This is the commonest pitfall met with in horsedealing. Indeed so common is it that it has almost come to be regarded as a normal act. It arises from temptation to enhance the value of a pony by easy means and in a manner which the prospective purchaser cannot readily verify for himself.

The regular practice is for a three year old to be described as a five year old; for an eight year old to be passed off as six and a fourteen year old to be shown as nine, and so on.

Yet it is possible to determine the age of a pony with a great degree of accuracy from one year to eight and thereafter, with a considerable degree of certainty, from eight to fifteen. The safeguard lies in requesting the veterinary surgeon examining the pony to record the age as nearly as he possibly can. Such forms part of the Examination for Identity already given.

In horse dealing it is permissible to describe any pony over eight years of age as 'Aged'. The term, however, is objectionable in that it is far too wide in its scope. The purchaser should insist upon a more definite interpretation of the age.

An incorrect statement of age, if made deliberately, can amount to fraud.

HEIGHT MEASUREMENT

Horse show and gymkhana classes for children are normally subdivided on height of ponies and it is here that height measurement assumes its chief importance. If a purchaser buys with the intention of showing the pony, he must ensure that it falls within the height limits of the class for which intended.

The safeguard lies in measurement being made accurately as part of the Examination as to Identity.

A scheme, known as the Joint Measurement Scheme, now operates whereby ponies, six years of age and over, are measured for life and a Life Certificate of Measurement granted. These certificates are accepted by nearly all Shows. A purchaser taking over a pony for which a Life Certificate of Measurement has been issued is entitled to claim the certificate also. The pitfall thus disappears if such a certificate exists.

OVERMOUNTING

By this is understood the mounting of a child on a pony beyond its capabilities. There are various aspects of the case. The pony may be unnecessarily big for the child, unduly strong for the child, or one that calls for a higher degree of control than the child is capable of. All constitute overmounting.

In the remounting of a child, however, some measure of overmounting is inevitable if experience is to be progressive. The child then grows into the pony in the same way that an allowance is made for growth in buying a child new clothes. A mistake arises only when the difference between the old pony the child is used to, and the new pony purchased in its place, is excessive.

UNDERMOUNTING

This is the reverse of the above; that is to say, mounting a child on a pony that is too small, not up to the weight to be carried and not equal to the work and pace the child merits. It results in waste of money and general disappointment.

UNSOUNDNESS

This is a highly technical matter and it is not made any easier through the fact that not all forms of unsoundness by any means necessitate rejection of the pony. The following is a brief résumé of the more common forms of unsoundness and their implications.

Vision.   Imperfect eyesight may mean anything from a quite insignificant defect to actual blindness of an eye. Yet in spite of such handicap the pony's performance may appear quite unaffected and the owner may not even know that vision is abnormal. In all cases the advice of the examining veterinary surgeon should be sought, for or against purchase.

A pony 'blind of an eye' is a danger in the face of oncoming or overtaking traffic on the affected side and unsafe in mounted games which involve a scramble.

Heart.   Heart disease is rare in ponies but if the heart action is reported as disordered in any way whatsoever, the pony should be rejected.

Wind.   The diseases known as Roaring and Whistling which are of such importance in horses are almost unknown in children's ponies and may be disregarded. On the other hand, Broken Wind, a tear of the lung structure, is all too common. Ponies so affected are incapable of sustained effort and show a chronic hollow cough.

So important is this condition that it is a sound rule *never to buy a coughing pony.*

Lameness. *Never buy a lame pony.* The lameness shown may be transient. On the other hand it may be chronic.

If the vendor insists that the lameness shown is temporary and of no consequence, then the correct procedure is to suspend the deal until such time as the vendor reports the pony as sound again.

Unsoundness causing lameness falls into two classes, namely, (1) sprains or strains and (2) bony enlargements.

Sprains affecting nerves or muscles are generally of little consequence. Those affecting tendons, ligaments and joints constitute a life-long weakness, the importance of which is in direct proportion to the severity of the original injury.

Bony enlargements are for the most part outgrowths of bone somewhere in the limbs, and horsemen employ an extensive vocabulary for them according to the part of the leg in which they appear. Those which encroach on joints must be regarded with suspicion. Those clear of joints are usually of less importance, unless lameness is shown.

A condition of great importance in children's ponies, particularly over-fat ponies, is that known as 'Laminitis' a disease of the feet resulting in life-long deformity and lameness. A pony which shows any evidence of having suffered in the past from this disease should be rejected without further question.

Skin Disease.   Contagious skin affections apart, there is only one skin disease in children's ponies which is of importance namely, that known as 'Sweet Itch'. This is an allergic skin condition which shows only during the summer months. A pony purchased in the winter may thus give no indication that he is a sufferer from this very distressing disease.

Wounds.   No one would knowingly buy a pony suffering from an extensive wound. It is the small wound which creates the problem. For instance, the pony under review may show a small stake wound, brushing wound or saddle gall, sustained the previous days, which the vendor states to be of no consequence. The correct procedure in such cases is for the prospective purchaser to inform the vendor in writing that he will buy the pony 'subject to the wound in question healing properly within the next ten days'. Payment is then delayed until the expiry of this period. Most vendors expect some such condition as this to be imposed and provided they are satisfied that the wound is trivial they will accept the conditions.

Rigs. Rigs are imperfectly castrated ponies. As such they have the characteristics of a stallion and are thus totally unsuitable for use by children.

Debilitation. *Never buy a thin pony.* The poor condition shown may be due to disease. On the other hand it may simply arise through neglect. Whatever the reason the purchaser will be involved in additional expense in putting matters right.

A thin pony purchased in winter time may be too poor to live out without cruelty and suffering.

———

PART V

A QUESTIONNAIRE

NO LIST OF QUESTIONS, however long, could possibly cover every contingency associated with buying a pony for a child. The following provides a check on the more important aspects of the problem.

THE CHILD

Have you a clear picture in mind as to what class of pony you want?

And is this identical with what the child really needs?

Do you possibly hold exaggerated ideas as to your child's abilities as a rider? (If so you are in danger of overmounting the child.)

Does the child like the pony you have found and does the child ride the pony with happiness and with confidence?

THE PONY

Class. Has the pony you have found any previous experience of the class of work for which you require him?

Have you been able to obtain any information as to his previous history and performance?

Did the present owner disclose his reason for parting?

Has the pony ever won any prizes in any class of event and if so how long ago?

Does he belong to any special breed and if so, has he a stud book registration number? (Important only where the intention is to exhibit the pony in breed classes.)

Has he been in regular work to date? (If not he may be above himself or out of hand. Or he may have been roughed off and rested for lameness.)

Height.   Is he about the height you had in mind for your child?

Has he been properly measured?

Does a Life Certificate of Measurement exist? (If so you are entitled to claim it.)

Will he be eligible for the show classes with a height restriction in which you propose to show him?

Age.   Is the pony about the age you prefer?

Has the age been verified?

Is he under 5 years of age? (If so your local Branch of the Pony Club may object to his use at rallies, at camp or for hunting.)

Is he old and past his prime and does this matter in your particular case?

Conformation.   Have you seen the pony?

Is the general appearance of the pony pleasing?

Is he too fat, too round, too tubby?

Is he narrow and flat-sided?

Will the use of a crupper prove necessary to keep the saddle in position?

Is he too thick or too short in the neck?

Action. How does he move? Is the action short and stumpy and does he raise his knees high?

Does he throw his feet well forward at all paces?

Does he go close in front or behind so as to hit himself? and are old brushing marks or wounds in evidence?

Is he lame?

Temperament. How did he behave when ridden for you?

Was any difficulty experienced in getting the bridle on?

Did he jib when asked to move on?

Did he fight the bridle, fret, fuss or take a hold of the bit?

Was he bitted severely or lightly for the trial?

Did he seem obedient and readily controllable at all paces?

And was he easy to pull up?

Was there any exhibition of bucking, rearing or shying?

And did you see him out in traffic?

How did he behave when your child rode him?

And did the child take a fancy to him and seem confident in the
saddle?

Did the child fall off and if so was it the child's fault or the pony's?

Will the owner consent to you taking the pony on a week's trial?

Keep.   Has the pony lived a stabled existence or has he been used
to liberty at grass?

Is he the sort that will live out?

Is he at present clipped?

Vice.   Is he easy to catch when turned loose at grass?

Will he live contentedly alone?

Does he kick or bite?

Does he kick out at hounds?

Will he enter a horse box or trailer quietly?

Is he easy to shoe?

Is he traffic proof?

Soundness.   Has he been submitted to veterinary examination?

And was he passed SOUND?

If not, to what extent do the disabilities revealed detract from
usefulness?

To what extent do they affect the price asked for the pony?

Does the question whatever arise as to whether he is Broken Winded?

Are the feet healthy and good and is the hoof free of cracks or breaks?

Is there any evidence that the pony has ever been a sufferer from the disease known as Laminitis?

Is the pony in good condition?

If a mare, is she in-foal?

———

PART VI

BRITISH BREEDS OF PONIES

GREAT BRITAIN IS RICH in her indigenous and other breeds of pony, alike in the number available, their variety and their suitability for children. By a remarkable chance the one nation really interested in riding for children has at its disposal the finest display of ponies in the world. Demand in this case did not create supply. Rather supply created demand and the success and rapid growth of the Pony Club is in no small measure due to the adequate number of excellent ponies available to its members.

THE MOORLAND BREEDS

The characteristic common to all the Moorland breeds of pony is that of hardiness and their ability to maintain themselves on poor keep. This makes them invaluable to parents since they can live out at all seasons of the year, thereby effecting a saving in labour and expense.

Shetland Ponies.   This is the smallest of the British breeds. These ponies are measured in inches and not in hands and their average height varies from 34 in. to 40 in.

Most Shetland ponies make excellent children's 'First Ponies' and instil confidence in the beginner both on account of their low height and slow pace. Others, however, prove mischievous and are sometimes too strong in the neck for a young child to control. Their chief fault is that they are inclined to run to fat so proving too broad for a small child to sit with comfort or security.

Dartmoor Ponies.   These small ponies vary in size from 11.00 to 12.00 hands. They make excellent mounts for small children when carefully broken and handled. They are of rather a nervous temperament and need careful schooling.

Exmoor Ponies.   These very attractive ponies vary in size from 12.00 to 12.2 hands. They make excellent children's ponies if broken carefully. They are strong and able to carry weight. Their chief fault is that they are inclined to be thick in the shoulder, but they include many first class ponies.

New Forest Ponies.   The average height of these ponies is from 12.2 to 13.2 hands but many attain a height of 14.2 hands if hand reared.

The great merit of these ponies is that they are invariably 'traffic proof'. In their natural habitat the mares graze along the verge of the main roads so that from birth the foals become accustomed to all forms of 'road nuisance'.

New Forest ponies are natural jumpers, docile, easily trained and sure footed. They make excellent children's ponies over a wide range of ages.

Welsh Riding Ponies.   These vary in height from 12.00 to 13.00 hands. They are very beautiful showy ponies with strong Arab characteristics though sometimes a little quick for the complete beginner. They are quite the prettiest of all the native breeds.

Dales and Fell Ponies.   The average height is 13.2 to 14.2 hands but they are more strongly built than the breeds previously considered. They are, perhaps, more suitable for older children or adults and are ideal for escort purposes.

Highlands Ponies.   Again a strongly built pony from 13.2 to 14.2 hands and more suitable for older children and adults.

Connemara Ponies.   This is Ireland's only native breed but they are readily obtainable in Britain. They vary in height from 13.2 to 15.00 hands. The lighter riding type is excellent for older children. A quality pony and a good all-round pony.

OTHER BREEDS

Hackneys.   Strictly speaking these are harness ponies. They seldom make good saddle ponies but occasionally an exception is found that jumps extremely well. They vary in height from 14.2 to 15.2 hands.

Arabs and Anglo-Arabs.   The characteristics of the Arab are natural beauty and untiring energy and these show strongly also in the cross-bred. These ponies are quick to learn and easy to train. They make excellent mounts for the more experienced rider.

Miniature Thoroughbreds.   These ponies are of uncertain origin but have much the appearance of a thoroughbred horse. They are of any size. If well trained and of the right temperament they excel in the show ring since inevitably they catch the judge's eye. In consequence of this they fetch high prices.

OTHER OFFICIAL PUBLICATIONS

British Horse Society Publications
"RULES FOR DRESSAGE"
"RULES FOR COMBINED TRAINING"
*"RIDING" by Mrs. V. D. S. Williams

Pony Club Publications
*"THE INSTRUCTORS' HANDBOOK"
*"THE MANUAL OF HORSEMANSHIP"
*"TRAINING THE YOUNG HORSE AND PONY"
*"KEEPING A PONY AT GRASS" by Mrs. O. Faudel-Phillips, F.I.H.
*"MOUNTED GAMES AND GYMKHANAS"
"QUIZ QUESTIONS"
*"POLO FOR THE PONY CLUB"
*"RIDING TO HOUNDS"
"NOTES FOR FIVE-MINUTE LECTURES—FOXHUNTING"
"THE PONY CLUB YEAR BOOK"

---

*"BASIC TRAINING FOR YOUNG HORSES & PONIES" by
Mrs. V. D. S. Williams
*"THE FOOT AND SHOEING" by Major C. Davenport, F.R.C.V.S.
"THE GENERAL PURPOSE SEAT" by Col. The Hon. C. G. Cubitt,
D.S.O., T.D., D.L. and Col. G. T. Hurrell, O.B.E.
*"BITS AND BITTING" by Col. The Hon. C. G. Cubitt
*"THE AIDS AND THEIR APPLICATION" by Col. The Hon. C. G. Cubitt
D.S.O., T.D., D.L.
Film Strips are also available for each of these titles

An up-to-date price list of Pony Club publications is shown in the
Pony Club Year Book, issued annually, and is available from Head-
quarters, address as below.

These and other publications connected with the horse are
available from

THE BRITISH HORSE SOCIETY
National Equestrian Centre, Kenilworth
Warwickshire, CV8 2LR

These are available from
BARRON'S
113 Crossways Park Drive
Woodbury, New York 11797